Confused Woman

Edited by Heidi Sheard
Layout and design by Kendal Marsh

Published by Confused Woman, LLC, 910 1st Street S. #5212, Hopkins, MN 55343

ISBN 978-0-692-56760-9

www.confusedwoman.com

Confused Woman

Tales & Advice on Love, Dating & Relationships

by Melanie Reitz

Introduction

Hello and thank you! If you made it to this point, I am ecstatic. Why? Well, because if you're reading this, you were intrigued enough by the cover or description of the book to open and hopefully purchase it. Please continue reading, enjoy the stories with additional commentary I have included just for you. As you will see, the good, the bad, and the ugly regarding dating, love, and relationships is alive and well in my world! I have a sneaking suspicion you've experienced similar situations as well. So, sit back, grab a cocktail, and immerse yourself in the madness of the real-life stories in *Confused Woman*.

Acknowledgments

To my Mare Bear, without you, I could not exist. You are the love of my life. To CF, for being the best boyfriend a woman could ever have. You have shown me that great guys really do exist and that finding your soul mate and best friend is possible. I love you, sexy. To my old neighbor Mike, without you, this book would never have happened. Thank you for the words of encouragement, incredible knowledge, and tasty cocktails. I owe you big time. Thanks to my family, especially Mom and Dad, for giving me an idyllic upbringing and allowing my creativity and sarcasm to run free. Thank you for always being supportive, even when you weren't 100% on board. To Crazy Uncle Terry, I've channeled you and miss you dearly. To Grandpa Henry, the king of sarcasm and the Polish Prince, I miss your smile and snarky comments every single day. Broadway Pizza sales in Nordeast will never be the same. Anne, what can I say, you're my sister from another mother. Love ya, bitch. To Diane, you are a second mom and awesome friend, not to mention the hottest grandma around! A big thank you to all of my girlfriends who I've shared all these stories with during walks and happy hours. You're the best. Love to you all! Finally, to all the men who traveled in and out of my love life, I could not have written a word of this without you. Thank you and best wishes to you all.

Table of Contents

Dating Tips and Tricks

No Fairy Tales Here

This happened when I was married to my daughter's father. I was recalling a previous bad dating experience, not realizing that I would someday find myself back in the dating pool again.

We've all experienced a dating nightmare...some more than others. There are the lucky ones (.0001% of the population) who find Mr. Right at the Sadie Hawkins dance in high school, get married, have 2.3 perfect kids, and live in blissful harmony for the rest of their days. Then there are the rest of us. I did not find Mr.

Right in high school or college. No fairytale romances here. I had a few good ones and plenty of bad ones.

One such horrible experience was when I was dating "a friend of a friend." He sounded good on paper and seemed nice enough. But after a few dates, the red flags started flying. Why doesn't he ever let me in his apartment? Why does he never drink alcohol? Is it because if he mixes it with his "mood-stabilizing" medication, bad things will happen? Is he a recovering alcoholic?

Around this time, I was selling my home and moving. This new and "interesting" boyfriend offered that he and his brother could drive the moving truck for me the next day. I could not say no to that. So, we loaded up the truck and then decided we should go out for dinner to celebrate our hard work. My boyfriend began to complain that he always had to drive and for once, he wanted me to drive so he could have a few drinks. This was completely fine and no big deal.

When we get to the restaurant, he immediately ordered an Iron Butterfly (I don't know what was in it, but it smelled nasty.) He ordered a second one and then a third one. I didn't think anything of it until his personality did a complete 180 and his evil twin appeared (we'll call him Damian).

At this point, I was annoyed. Through clenched teeth, I threatened to leave him at the restaurant if we didn't leave ASAP. He got into my car (barely) and was gagging the entire

He sounded good on paper and seemed nice enough. But after a few dates, the red flags started flying.

ride home. Luckily it was a short drive. No sooner did we arrive, he puked and passed out on my front lawn. Great. To top it off, my neighbors across the street were police officers. Brilliant.

I somehow got him to wake up and crawl up to my front porch where he started crying like a baby and told me his depressing life story. After that thrilling therapy session, I got him into the house where he spent the rest of the night alternating between the toilet and the tile floor, praying for mercy.

The next day, Damian's brother showed up and convinced me he was able to drive the moving truck by himself to my new home which was over an hour away. As I waved goodbye, I wondered if I'd ever see my belongings again.

My belongings made it, but needless to say, I didn't see Damian ever again. I didn't even go on another date for a while. No thanks!

Dating Hell

My former co-worker and friend is a wonderful person, but extremely naïve when it comes to dating. The red flags were flying, but she was walking by them like a blind squirrel.

G one are the days of thumping melons in the produce department while a hot guy looks at you like you are a nut case. Since we are such a digital society nowadays, people rarely meet dating hopefuls face-to-face. We have turned to the internet and dating websites, which for better or for worse, is the most commonly used method to "meet" the opposite gender.

I must admit, in my single days, I did turn to those sites. It was fun to sit in the privacy of my own home and peruse the

On the way to the coffee shop, she asked me, "Do you think it's weird that he makes a living selling knives on eBay?"

sites with a drink in hand, free to either gush over or slam the men and their profiles. More often than not, their photos were at least five years old and twenty pounds thinner than the real thing.

As exciting as it was online, it was always disastrous in person. The guy looked nothing like the photo and never lived up to the fairytale package he created on his page. There were many times I would be sitting in a restaurant or coffee shop and watch a guy come in and think, *Please don't be him. Keep walking, keep walking...oh no...he's coming right towards me. Quick, hide behind the menu!*

I have a dear friend who is divorced with two children. Ever since her new-found freedom, she's been actively pursuing male companionship. So, when my friend told me she was looking on these sites for a man I thought, *Oh no...here we go...creep alert.* The first of her guys I met by accident. She and I were going out for drinks one night, but she made the mistake of telling this guy what restaurant we were going to. We were having a great girls night when all of a sudden, this guy appears out of nowhere with a dozen roses. I thought someone was peddling them to make a buck but no, they were from "Mr. Wonderful." *What a dork*, I thought.

After I made a quick exit, I emailed her and said she may want to look elsewhere. But no, she thought he was her knight in shining armor. That was until he started getting angry every time she wanted to go out without him. I warned her he was controlling and to run away, but she didn't listen. It wasn't until he "magically" appeared at a restaurant just minutes after she told him the location that she got the hint he was a controlling psycho.

I thought that after that fiasco, my friend would turn to the produce department but alas, no. She continued to check out the dating websites and found "Mr. Fabulous." He said all the right things and was very interested in her. She wanted me to meet him and get my opinion. On the way to the coffee shop, she asked me, "Do you think it's weird that he makes a living selling knives on eBay?"

What?! I thought she was joking but she was serious. After I picked my jaw up off the ground, she tried to make it sound better by adding, "They aren't just any knives, they're antique knives." Oh, so that makes it better. *Whew! Is she nuts?* Antique or not, knives kill. If he was selling sweaters and baseball hats on eBay, I could maybe give him a chance but knives? Hell to the no!

Needless to say, I told her to move on and stay away from the knife-selling crazy man. Let's hope the next time she introduces me to a man, he is in the checkout lane with a nice watermelon in hand.

Coffee, Tea & Me?

Ah, my flight attendant days. What an absolute blast! Granted, there were some sucky times, but for the most part, it was an awesome experience. There are so many stories to share, but the male passenger and pilot encounters were the best...and the most interesting.

have several friends who are either getting divorced or are divorced. We regularly have venting sessions about their dating horrors, which brings me back to the time when I was a flight attendant. I was single then and could not believe the number of pilots and passengers, married and unmarried, who would hit on me.

The male passengers who were quite friendly were usually between the ages of thirty and seventy. They were almost always consuming alcohol and thought they were the cat's meow. Some of them actually weren't too bad but most were not going to be on anyone's Top Ten list anytime soon. Most were either very curious, horny, or both. They would press the call button many times, sometimes for drinks, always for attention. They would ask: "What's it like being a flight attendant? Have you ever been in the cockpit? What exactly do they do up there? Can you ask the captain (usually during takeoff or landing) the score of the football game?"

The worst offenders, however, were the pilots. I had heard stories about how pilots were flirtatious and unfaithful, but I was shocked at how true it actually was. I would fly several routes a day and on at least one of those flights or hotel overnights, I would be hit on. On one particular trip, I went out to dinner with some pilots. After we returned to the hotel, I received a phone call from the co-pilot who was a married man. He asked if I'd like to come to his hotel room to "hang out." I also had another pilot who happened to have an adjoining room to mine. He kept knocking on the door, wondering if I would like to come over to watch TV. Uh huh, right.

Seriously, guys, what's the deal? It's not like I'm Jennifer Aniston or Angelina Jolie. Maybe it was the uniform? Maybe it was the fact I give out free pretzels? All I know is that it was

They were almost always consuming alcohol and thought they were the cat's meow.

crazy. The attention at first was fun, but after a while, it grew old and later, downright annoying. I felt like a piece of meat that was being drooled over by a pack of wolves.

I now work an office job...not nearly as exciting and no drooling men, but at least I don't have to worry about getting propositioned every ten minutes or having a kid barf on me!

Swimming in the Dating Pool Again

My ex-husband and I were separated. I was so pissed when I saw a profile picture of him and my daughter on match.com. We were still married, and he was out trolling for dates. So, out of spite, I created a profile as well. It was the beginning of an interesting adventure, to say the least.

hen my husband and I decided to divorce, it was sad, but both necessary and amicable. We would both be better off, we decided. It was hard on

The guys actually seemed normal and didn't look like they should be on death row.

our daughter at first, but in the end, I would rather have her see two healthy parents on their own than two people miserable in a marriage. I would never want her to think our relationship is a model for a successful and happy union.

That being said, I had to do the dreaded...get back into the dating game. Ugh. I would rather have signed up for several root canals than go on a date with some creep. It had been several years, so I was a little rusty. I decided to check out match.com for the hell of it to see what is out there...OMG.

I put my profile out there with the cutest picture I could find. Within minutes I was bombarded with "winks" and "likes." *Cool*, I thought, until I checked out who was doing the winkin' and the likin'. All scary. Two were from Colorado and Los Angeles, which I guessed were scam artists, so I immediately deleted those. One had no photo and was from a local city known for its state prison. Gone. The others were guys that either looked like they should be incarcerated or they could be my grandpa. Yuck!

I was simultaneously turned off and depressed.

So, this is what my dating life will be? Full of scary, creepy perverts looking for a piece? No thanks. I'd rather stay home and watch reruns of the *Real Housewives of Beverly Hills*. Hell, I'd rather watch paint dry than date losers like that.

The next day, I thought I would take another look at my profile. I was surprised to see a couple that weren't so scary.

The guys actually seemed normal and didn't look like they should be on death row. They sent nice emails, nothing sick or twisted, so I thought why not just say "Hi." What could it hurt? It's not like they know my name or where I live. It is all very secretive...I feel like I'm on a covert dating operation.

Turns out both guys were nice and not weird. It gave me the confidence to keep emailing and maybe down the road, chat on the phone or meet for coffee. I'm not ever going to meet anyone shutting myself off from the outside world, but I'm not going to be stupid and be an open book either. In fact, I kind of enjoyed the whole mysterious undercover thing. Maybe I'd go by Lana and sport a wig and sunglasses on the first meeting.

Warning: There are Perverted Sharks in the Pool

Ahh..the joys of online dating. It's amazing the amount of scum looking for sex. I thought for a while I was on CreepsAndPervsWhoNeedSexDesperately.com.

ow. That is all I have to say after my first week on match.com. I cannot tell you the amount of creepy perverts who "winked" at me or messaged me. Yuck. I seriously felt like I needed to take a shower after being on my computer.

They barely say "Hi" before they tell me how sexy my photo looks. Really? Do these jerks think I am that stupid to fall for a "Hey, Sexy" comment? Ugh. It was a complete turnoff and I was quick to block these perverts. I think match.com is a total meat market and I was the prey.

However, I did manage to find a couple of guys that genuinely seemed nice. The one I did talk to on the phone went on and on about his nasty divorce. I don't mind someone talking about it for a few minutes but for an hour? It was too much drama and too depressing for me.

The other guy seemed very nice and has a daughter not much older than mine. We made plans to meet for a glass of wine and I was so nervous, my stomach was in knots. I felt like I was back in high school again, hoping the cute boy would ask me out. In this case, I hoped we wouldn't discuss our exes for two hours.

I Survived the Swim

Ugh, the dreaded first date after being off the market almost six years. Let the games begin!

survived. I was such a nervous wreck all day and up until the moment I was escorted to the table at the restaurant. It is one thing to see pictures and to chat with someone via e-mail, but quite another to meet him in person. Will he live up to the pictures? Will he be as friendly as the emails? Will he be a complete jerk?

I was pleasantly surprised that he resembled his photos! The conversation flowed smoothly (which explains why we were at the restaurant for three and a half hours) and he asked me lots of *normal* questions. I was waiting for the conversation to get all weird and perverted, but it never did. We actually talked a lot about our kids, our childhood, our likes/dislikes, and what we hoped for the future.

It was a great evening. I have to say it was very nice to have someone treat me to dinner and not complain about how much it cost. I met someone who actually walked me to my car and said they enjoyed my company. For the first time in a long time, I felt important and attractive.

We exchanged many texts after that date. He wanted to see me again and the feeling was mutual. Even if I didn't go out with this man again, I was looking forward to having my independence. No more answering to another person.

This was a huge turning point for me. After divorce, no matter how broken you feel, you can date again. You are worthy of finding the perfect person for you!

Hello?

Ah, the ups and downs of dating. I was convinced I would meet the man of my dreams on match. com, yet that is exactly what didn't happen.

The first date went very well! The following two nights, we texted for several hours. Things were looking good for a next date. He seemed very interested. And then... silence. No texting, no phone calls for two days. I figured he was probably busy with his daughter, with whom he had fifty percent custody.

At the end of the second day of silence, I sent a friendly text wishing him a happy weekend. He quickly replied, saying he was going to call me the other night but was too busy. Hmmm.

I decided to give him the weekend with his daughter and was sure I would hear from him the following Monday.

Nope. Nothing. It was so bizarre. We had a great time, texted for hours, and then zilch. I don't get it. For someone that seemed so into me, it made no sense why all of a sudden there was no communication. *Did he find someone else? Did he change his mind about me? Is he lazy and expects me to chase him?* I started wondering if I texted something crazy or weird that would have turned him off? Nope. Nothing.

What the hell?! This dating thing is so frustrating. You think things are great and then all of a sudden they're not. I decided to forget about Mr. Potential and turn my focus onto other things. Why put myself through a roller coaster ride? Granted, match.com is entertaining, but it is certainly not going to be the "end all be all" for finding the man of your dreams. It is a fun place to check out the eye candy and cringe at the creeps. Friday nights never looked so good, right?

Lazy or Delusional?

I seriously doubt most men actually read the online dating profiles. I'm pretty sure they either pursue or pass based on the photo. Gee, I wonder which protruding body part is running the show?

U gh, the dreaded internet dating. I swore I would never do it again, but there I was, in the cyber world of dating hell. You see the match.com ads and you think, "Wow, maybe I really can find a decent guy online!" Then you log on.

I swear every creepy, disgusting, perverted weirdo on match. com somehow finds their way to your profile. I sent out a ton of "winks" and emails to normal-looking guys, hoping for a response, but in the end, heard nothing but crickets.

I know I'm not Megan Fox, but I'm certainly not a troll either. So, I have come to the conclusion that these idiots on match are either lazy or delusional. They are lazy because they don't want to take the time to pursue women, expecting they will come running to them because they are oh–so-fabulous (insert finger down throat here). They are delusional because they are glancing at profiles and expecting a Jennifer Aniston or a JLo when ninety-nine percent of us either never did, don't now, and never will look like *that*.

You are assessed by a couple of photos you put on the site and do most men even bother to read your profile? No. They instantly judge you by the pictures and decide you are not worth pursuing. I felt like chopped liver in the internet meat market.

I decided I'd be better off thumping melons at the grocery store than acting like I knew all about football while admiring the big screen TV's at Best Buy. I needed to end the madness and abandon online dating sites for a while. The frustration and lunacy of it all drove me to look for other ways to find and pursue available men.

Too Good to be True

I did it. I met the "Hot Hawaiian." For real. He was gorgeous, smart, and an amazing kisser. Too bad he was also a narcissistic prick.

The minute I decided to take a break from all the delusional and lazy men on match.com, good men started appearing. So back in the saddle I went...

A man "winked" at me. I saw his picture and thought, *hmmm... not really my type*. I was about to delete him when something made me take a second look. I checked out his profile and he actually sounded great: Forty-five years old, very athletic, father to one twelve-year-old son, owns his own law firm, and is originally from Hawaii. *Heaven on Earth*, I said to myself.

This is awesome! It's not every day you find someone who is cute and employed! So, I decided to "wink" back. He followed up with an email saying he was very interested in meeting me. We arranged to meet the next night at a restaurant. I was a nervous wreck and hoped for the best.

I walked in and was pleasantly surprised. I can honestly say his picture didn't do him justice. He was gorgeous and in fantastic shape. We instantly hit it off and ended up talking for four and a half hours. It was a great time and the goodbye kiss was insane. I thought, *This is it, here's the man of my dreams.*

That's when paranoia kicked in. *Is this guy too good to be true? Can he really be a lawyer? Does he really run all these races? Did he really attend these schools and obtain these degrees?*

I started to panic and scoured the internet looking for any information I could find on him. Hell, I even did a free background check to see if he had a criminal past. I remembered he paid with cash the night we met, so I saw neither a driver's license nor a credit card with his name on it. *What if that wasn't even his name? Could he be one of those impostors who dupes unsuspecting women like I heard about on "Dateline?"*

I had to shut it down or I'd lose my mind.

It got to the point where I was driving myself insane with worry. I had to shut it down or I'd lose my mind. Turns out it really wasn't necessary, since he stood me up for lunch a couple of days later. He apologized twice, saying his meeting ran late, but I didn't know if I could believe him. I really knew it was a bunch of crap when he said he'd contact me to set up another time to meet and I never heard back.

So, I decided once again to take a break from the 'ole match.com and put the brakes on the dating thing. I had a love/hate relationship with the website. It was clear to me I was not ready if I was taking every little rejection so personally and feeling paranoid that every guy is either a serial killer or a con artist. Cable TV, here I come!

The Bubonic Plague of Online Dating

How come I felt like a carnival freak as I perused online profiles while men get to feel like they are seeking a "real" woman? Everyone knows what they really want is a bimbo with a big rack and a nice ass.

Well...I came to the conclusion that I was indeed the bubonic plague of online dating. Why, do you say? Well, I'll tell you why.

One weekend, I decided to be assertive and peruse profiles on match.com. If the men seemed interesting, I gave them a "wink" or sent them a message. I found a dozen that seemed at least worthy of a casual conversation. The "winks" and messages were sent and how many responded? ....a big fat ZERO.

That's right ladies and gentlemen, not a one so much as moved his eyelashes in my direction. I heard crickets, it was so silent. Now, I am not a supermodel, but who is? You would think out of the dozen contacts, I would hear something back....

After several hours of heavy thought, aided by comfort foods and beverages, I came to the conclusion that men are looking for Barbie. They don't want a real woman with real curves and a personality. A mute, arm trophy is the ideal date of the week. Ugh!

So, what do we normal women do when so many men are looking for the impossible and the imbecilic? Well, we turn to cable TV and put aside our hopes and dreams that there are guys out there who look beyond the superficial and appreciate us for who we are under our epidermis. For the male dolts out there, that means skin!

It Could be so Much Worse

I love my friend, Diane. She is a feisty and fun "mature woman" who has a knack for falling into horrific dating situations. Sorry, Diane, but I am still laughing about this one!

went out for drinks and appetizers on a Friday night with my dear friend, Diane. We went to Murray's, which is an excellent steakhouse in Minneapolis. For those of you who've never been, I highly suggest you check it out. Murray's has my new favorite appetizer, The Frickle, a gourmet fried pickle. It's to die for!

Diane and I began discussing, okay, bitching about our dating woes. She has been single for several decades and has suffered bad dates innumerable times. I told her I was the bubonic plague of online dating and she told me to shut up.

Diane pulled out her phone and showed me the men that have contacted her recently on Ourtime.com, a dating site for those fifty and older. Diane is sixty-five but looks and acts much, much younger. It's good and bad. It's good because she looks great and is a hell of a lot of fun to hang out with. It's bad because the guys that are her age look like they're knocking on Heaven's door.

I couldn't help but laugh at the look of disgust on her face as she showed me these fossils and their corresponding profiles. One after another...it was like a zombie pictorial. All of a sudden, I didn't feel so bad. I may be the bubonic plague, but at least I'm not getting hit on by the walking dead!

The Things I do for Dates

This is so typical of me. I am really hot for someone, so I say I like something, when in reality, it is the last thing on earth I want to do. Gee, I wonder why it never works out?

Yes, I am one of those...someone who will tell a potential date, "I've never jumped from a fifty-story building before, but gee, that sure sounds like fun!" Okay, maybe not always to that extreme, but I am very willing to try something I know damn well I'll hate just for the sake of going out with someone.

The thought of being on a motorcycle scares me to death, but the guy was cute so the truth escaped me.

For example, I met a guy from match who was going rollerblading with his teenage daughters. Have I ever wanted to Rollerblade? No. Was I going to give it a try so I could pretend I actually had something in common with this guy? Yes.

I brought my daughter, who has also never bladed before.

The guy and his daughters were nice enough, but we couldn't really talk since my daughter and I were hugging the wall the entire time. I was so worried about her or myself falling that I couldn't even form complete sentences. All that came out of my mouth was, "Whoa! Are you okay?" Under my breath, I was cursing and saying, "When will this be over? This better get me a second date!" Alas, there was no second date. Big surprise!

Another time, I tried to impress a guy by telling him I also loved riding motorcycles. What a load of crap. The thought of being on a motorcycle scares me to death, but the guy was cute so the truth escaped me. For our first date, Mr. Wonderful picked me up on his motorcycle. I put on a brave face and acted like I was so excited to go for a ride. Inside, I was a complete wreck. We barely made it down the street, going 30 mph at best, when I started whimpering like a little girl and asked if we could turn around.

He was nice enough to go back and get his car, but by then it was too late. It was obvious I had lied. The date was over before it started.

I decided that from that day forward, I would not agree to any unfamiliar sports or dangerous activities unless I sincerely wanted to try them. Of course, if Ben Affleck's clone walks through my front door, I will tell him I've always wanted to climb Mount Kilimanjaro!

Shopping for a Sugar Daddy

I couldn't resist checking this out, thanks to my crazy, former co-worker. Love ya, Jeb!

Yet again, I had just about given up on match.com. What a joke. If you're a whore, it's a great place to meet a guy. I, however, was looking for a relationship with a little more substance than, "Drop 'em."

My co-workers and I were joking about dating sites when one of them mentioned sugardaddie.com. He told me it's a legitimate site that's been featured on Dr. Phil. Men that are financially well-off use the site to find women to date and hopefully marry.

Stupidity ruled over the wallet and I decided to go for it.

This was too tempting for me not to investigate! Curiosity (and a few beers) got the best of me that night, and I checked out the site. There were men, from their upper thirties to their late seventies from all over the country (and even the United Kingdom), who were looking for the woman of their dreams.

As a half-joke, I thought, why not create a profile and see what happens? So, I did just that and waited. The next day, I was surprised and a little scared to see a half dozen responses. Of course, to read their e-mails, I'd have to pay for at least one month of membership.

Stupidity ruled over the wallet and I decided to go for it. So, there I was a member of sugardaddie.com. Seriously!

A few of the responses were notifications that I was being placed on someone's "hotlist." Okay, whatever. Another couple of guys had profiles but no pictures so I immediately deleted them, figuring they were either cheating husbands, drug dealers, or downright ugly.

The two messages I did read were not too bad. One man was from the Twin Cities, in his late forties, single, and obviously well off. He was looking for someone to share cocktails and dinners. If nothing else, I thought, *This will be awesome blog material!* Besides, if he takes me to some swanky place, it will more than pay for the cost of the site membership fee. I responded...but never heard back.

The next message was from a man who was in his late fifties and lived in Texas. Two strikes off the bat...old and distance. However, he seemed very nice, financially stable, and didn't look half-bad for an old guy. I decided to respond and see what he had to say. He told me how wonderful he was and that he'd show me the world, buy me presents, and treat me like a princess. Wow, sounded good! He sent some photos, including one of him in Paris...I was intrigued.

The man from Texas said all the right things and sounded nice, so I thought, why not give him a chance. I responded and sent a couple additional photos of myself. I heard nothing. I'm guessing he copy and pasted the letter to ten other women and when my photo didn't meet his expectations, he moved on. Wait, the dude's an old fart on sugardaddie.com and you're judging me?!

The site didn't quite pan out like I was hoping it would...but it was very interesting. Maybe next time, I should send some photos from my spring break trip in college and see if I get a response.....or maybe it would give him a heart attack!

D Day

Divorce Day. It sucked. At the same time, I can honestly say that everyone is much better off. No child should live in a home full of anger and sadness. My daughter now has two homes full of love, happiness, and most importantly, peace.

F inally, it was the light at the end of the tunnel. May 22 was "D Day" for me. That's the day we met with the judge to get the divorce finalized. It was fairly casual since we didn't involve the money-grabbing lawyers. It was just us and the judge. It only took the judge twenty minutes to sign the papers. There was no crying, no arguing, just the facts and the signature of approval.

Of course, it wasn't "official" until we got the dissolution letter in the mail. For all practical purposes, the minute the judge signed off and dismissed us, it was final. The marriage that started out so promising was killed by the formal pen stroke of a judge we had never met.

We parted at the elevators---the awkward hug between two ex-spouses. He said, "Thanks for going on this journey with me." All I could do is say, "Yep, it's been interesting." He mentioned still being friends and to feel free to reach out for help regarding our daughter at any time. I nodded and smiled while I thought, *You weren't there before when you were legally bound to be and now you're suddenly going to be there? We shall see.*

I walked away from the courthouse feeling a little numb and dazed, but amazingly at peace.

I had mixed emotions. The first reaction was "Finally!" The second reaction was a rush of sadness. I feel badly for my daughter who won't grow up with Mom and Dad under the same roof. At the same time, I don't want her living with a mom and dad who fight constantly.

In some ways, I feel like the divorce is a sign of failure, while at other times I feel like the divorce is a victory. I'm sad we couldn't get along and make it work, but I'm very happy I have a second chance at happiness. It's an opportunity to begin a new chapter in my life and look forward to what that will bring.

We parted at
the elevators—
the awkward hug
between two
ex-spouses.

When the judge rubber stamped the papers, it was tough for me to fight back the tears. I had plans the next few nights to "celebrate" with friends. The sadness and mourning was only a part of what I was feeling. I also had a tremendous feeling of relief over my new-found freedom. I wanted to take time to discover myself and plan for my new future. I hoped that someday, I would find someone who is truly a good fit for me. No more lousy, dysfunctional relationships for me! Cheers!

Can Sex be Better Than a Root Canal?

Nothing sucks more than bad sex, and Lord knows I've had plenty of it. It was so refreshing to find CF and be attracted to him, both physically and mentally. That's what makes the sex so damn hot.

W e've all heard of great sex, but how many of us have actually had it? You may think you've had good sex, but then you find someone else and it's a mind-blowing experience. And you think, *Wow, now this is why people love to have sex!*

Hopefully, you've all experienced how great it can be. If not, my condolences. There's nothing like it. Trust me. I've had many pathetic, mediocre, yawn-inducing, and downright comatose experiences. They'll ask, "How was it?" while I'm thinking, *You really don't want to know how awful it was so I'll lie and tell you it was fabulous. Truth is, I'd rather have a root canal.*

I don't know what it is about guys, but they all think they're amazing in bed, when only about five percent of them truly are. The rest are either in deep denial or watch too much cable. To them, foreplay is simply stating, "Hey, wanna get it on?"

I've now found someone who not only gets it, but is actually good at it. He is more worried about my satisfaction than his. This, my friends, is a rarity. After years of having not-so-great sex, it's refreshing to not only have it be fabulous, but to have someone who actually cares how it was for me.

So, good luck to you all in your search for the next big "O" and just remember, if he can't give it to you, there's always a six-pack and the battery-operated friend....It can't get you pregnant and it can't give you an STD. It won't ask you if you'll be done before the last inning of the baseball game either.

Hot Doc Magnet

I don't know what it is, but I always get the hot, young, male resident doctors. Having a hot doctor finger me with a rubber glove in a totally non-sexual way? I think I will pass.

Well, they're not quite doctors yet, but for some reason I get all the male residents checking out my privates. Of course, they are not your average docs in training...Oh no...It's the "Zesty Italian Hotter-Than-Hell" doc who is just finishing up his residency. Let me explain.

The first time this happened, I had just given birth to my daughter. I needed to be sewn up. Who comes in to do the needlework? Not some sweet, innocent female resident with a 4-H mastery in quilting. Nope. I get Dr. McDreamy in training. That's exactly who I want down south in the region that looks like it's been through a food processor.

The second time this happened, I was at an OB/GYN appointment. I had an issue and needed to get in right away. The only doctor available was a male. Not a huge deal. I prefer a female doctor, but I needed to be seen.

Not only was he an hour late, but the nurse informed me he's a teaching doctor, so he has a resident shadowing him today and wondered if that would be okay. Great. What am I supposed to say? I groan and say okay, but secretly I'm thinking, *Wonderful. Now I'll have two strange guys checking out my va jay jay.*

There was a knock on the door and my stomach tied in a knot. The OB/GYN basically looked like a dad/grandpa. Okay, so far so good. The resident appeared from behind the doc. He looked like Ben Affleck's twin. Ugh! What is it with me and these hot residents? Why can't I get some totally nerdy doctor?

What is it with me and these hot residents? Why can't I get some totally nerdy doctor?

The exam went fine. It was kind of weird, though, when the doctor performed the internal exam and then turned to the resident and said, "Your turn."

Next time, I'm asking for the female doctor and if there's a male resident, he better look like Shrek.

Damaged Dudes

CF, you might have been a damaged dude, but I'm proud of you for the way you are overcoming the yuck. You are worth so much more than that!

Hi. From the bottom of my heart, brain, and self-esteem, I personally want to thank every woman who treated her ex-boyfriend/ex-fiance/ex-husband like complete crap. Thanks to you, nearly every guy I've dated post-divorce has been a damaged dude.

Sometimes, it's easy to spot the wounded man. The first date starts great but by the time you have a drink and appetizer, he's given you every dirty little detail of his breakup. They usually don't realize it's too much information until you excuse yourself to go to the bathroom and don't come back.

Other guys won't reveal that they are damaged goods until several dates later. There are small tidbits or comments that may hint at a wounded ego, but the bulk of it doesn't surface until you visit the wrong restaurant or the city they last lived in with "evil woman," that the ugly truth emerges.

The one that hurts the most is when you're really connecting and he leads you to believe everything is great. Then out of the blue, several months later, he states, "I don't ever want to get married again. I'm okay being alone." Wow...really? Then why the hell are you here with me?!

All I can think is, *What on earth did this woman do to damage you for life?* Besides pulling a Lorena Bobbitt and chopping off your wienie or draining your bank account, what could possibly be so horrible you wouldn't give a great woman a chance? Are you being a chicken or using it as a convenient excuse?

Oh, and to "those" women...well, you can just suck it. To CF, you are one in a million.

Alone Again

This was such a bad night, it hurts to retell the story. CF, I know you did what you had to do, but it still sucked.

signed up for a triathlon with a friend. The mental and physical preparation was a struggle, but I was doing it! Unfortunately, my friend had to withdraw due to a medical issue. I totally understood her situation, but it bummed me out. I was counting on her to be there with me during the triathlon.

I felt better after talking to representatives from the triathlon. They assured me I could complete the race and told me not be afraid. I came back around to a great attitude...I was in a good place...until that night.

My boyfriend had to suddenly commit to taking his son in for the weekend. I understand he had little choice, but it was a shock to my plans, since it was last minute and I was planning on his support during the triathlon. It wasn't my boyfriend's fault, but it still sucked.

The Honeymoon is Over

Oh, the first fight. What's worse, it made me admit that our relationship was not actually perfect. The fight was about something so incredibly stupid too. We both look back at this and laugh. It was so ridiculous and trivial, but yet it brought home the point that we're all human. Thankfully, we've only had a couple minor arguments since then, which is not too damn shabby, considering my ex-husband and I argued daily. I definitely do not miss that!

The sarcasm turned to hurt feelings which turned into an argument.

Y ou know how it is when you first start dating. Everything is great....the conversation, the nights out, the sex...all amazing...and then it happens... the first fight.

I had dinner with my boyfriend on a Friday night at one of our favorite restaurants out on their beautiful patio. It was a perfectly warm evening in September, which is a rare treat in Minnesota.

Saturday morning was nice as well. Despite the rain, we managed to fit in almost ninety minutes of tennis. We had a good workout and an even better time. Then the evening came.

I arrived at his house in the late afternoon, feeling the satisfaction of a productive, yet relaxing day. I was excited to see him. It started out fine, despite him being on a work call on a Saturday night. After he hung up, we joked around with each other, except the joking went too far. You see, we are both extremely sarcastic people which works well....sometimes. This time it triggered a fight.

The sarcasm turned to hurt feelings which turned into an argument. After some time, he apologized and everything was good in his world. However, on my end, I was still upset. This lasted another couple of hours until we were both at a place to talk about it.

The shattering of the "perfect" image of your boyfriend brings you back to reality. Alas, the dating honeymoon is over.

If you can put up with the not-so-great and appreciate the good qualities, then you've found the right person and a real relationship!

Caveman Communication

I love you, CF, but you are definitely not the best initiator of phone calls or texts. Sex, yes. Remote communication, no. You're hot as hell, so you are forgiven.

Ahhh....the joy of communicating with men. Are we asking too much when we expect them to initiate a dialogue? Is it really that hard to call or text now and then?

Case in point. My boyfriend, who is not the best at texting or calling, will talk non-stop if you are sitting in the same room with him. Put a phone in front of him and he'll clam up. It's like he's put on mute and his fingers are paralyzed!

After months of frustration with his lack of initiation, I decided to not text or phone first, just to see how long it would take him to contact me. I know this sounds completely childish, but I was frustrated, so cut me some slack.

Three days later, he finally texted me, "Hi there, how's it going?" Nice! He initiated conversation...this is good!

I responded and said, "I'm great. How was your weekend?" He answered but didn't ask how my weekend was or ask any questions to continue the conversation.

So, since there was no question to respond to, I decided to ask another question. Yet again, another answer, but no question in return. Ugh! Really? How do you keep up a conversation when it's one-sided? Then I realized he's probably glued to the baseball playoffs that were on TV.

I decided at that point to stop texting and go to bed. The next morning, I texted, "Good morning. Sorry for falling asleep on our conversation last night."

Put a phone in front of him and he'll clam up.

He texted back and said, "No worries. I figured you must have dozed off." Seriously? Wow. I guess that was his idea of a conversation but clearly not mine. He was grunting and nodding on the other end of the phone and I was jumping up and down, hoping for some attention.

Some guys are better at communicating than others, but don't be surprised or frustrated if this happens to you. Some things will never change.....

Mind Young! Body Not!

To this day, I am still working on accepting that my body is not a young body anymore. It's very frustrating to have to discipline myself in ways I never used to, but I have no choice. If I keep acting like a twenty-five-year-old, my body will not last. I want to be around for the long haul, to see my daughter grow up and have her own family. I don't want to be drooling on my grandchildren when they visit me at the nursing home. It's an ongoing motivator to keep my shit together!

n my early forties, I began to realize that my mind had a lot
of catching up to do with my body. Mentally, I was still back
in college, wanting to stay up all night partying and eating
like crap. Physically, I was not even close to those times.

Here was my proof. I would ache for days after a strenuous
workout. I would gain five pounds just by looking at junk
food. Party all night? Forget about it. Too many drinks
and I was a train wreck, all tired out and sick as a dog. What
happened? Where did that young person go?

Well, I'll tell you where this young person went. She grew up,
got married, started a career, divorced, continued career,
married, had a child, divorced, and ended up single again.
Whew! It exhausts me just to talk about it!

After my first divorce, I could handle going out on the town
and whooping it up. The second time around, I could barely
stay awake past 10:00 pm and would feel like death warmed
over for days after a night of drinking.

It was hard to grasp the thought of getting older. Heck, it's
still hard! However, I realize that I don't necessarily even
want to do all the things I did when I was younger. It's time
to move on and embrace the next chapter...one aspirin and
squirt of Ben Gay at a time.

Elevator Envy

This was a funny moment. CF was jealous and pissed. He could not believe I was the one who was in the elevator. It would be like CF walking into an elevator with Ben Affleck. I would be beyond envious! Sorry, CF.

My boyfriend and I went to see Toad the Wet Sprocket. If you have no clue who they are, you're not alone. I knew a handful of their songs, which were all on albums from the 1990's. The song I was most familiar with was from the *Friends* soundtrack and is titled "Good Intentions." It's a great song and I was very happy to hear it at the concert. But, of course, they also played many songs I was not familiar with.

My boyfriend is a huge fan and has followed them from the beginning. He knew every lyric for every song. I stood there, watched, and drank beer. Normally I would be bored to tears if I didn't know the majority of a band's music, but I wasn't because they were actually *really* good.

After the show, we headed over to a hotel bar a couple blocks away to have more drinks and some food. Since I'd had several beers and given birth to a child, I needed to go to the bathroom every fifteen minutes. I know that's a little too much information....sorry!

However, because of said bladder condition, I had to use the restroom which is on another floor of the hotel. As I entered the elevator, the musicians from Toad the Wet Sprocket stepped in after me. I couldn't believe it!

Part of me wanted to get off on their floor and try to strike up a conversation with them, but I thought that would be a little too creepy. So I used the restroom and rushed back to the table to tell my boyfriend the story of my elevator ride.

To say he was green with envy was an understatement. The next morning, he was still going on about it. What was I supposed to do, not tell him?!

Forever Connected

Divorced but forever connected. I don't mind, except for the times he's rude and argumentative, which reminds me why I divorced him in the first place. Good guy, good dad, not-so-great husband. I am very grateful we are friends and can get along for our daughter's sake.

always knew when I divorced, that my ex-husband and I would keep contact because we have a daughter together. However, I didn't realize that there would be other awkward interactions or situations, such as the "Divorce Chauffeur."

At this point, I figured my obligation was done. Wrong.

The ordeal began on a Sunday afternoon when his truck battery died. He was supposed to drop off our daughter but couldn't because of the said battery failure. He asked if I could give him a jump. Being the nice gal that I am, I said yes.

His truck was parked in an underground parking garage, full of cement pillars and cars. I had just purchased my car a few months before...brand, spanking new. I was nervous to drive it on an open freeway, let alone in a dark, narrow parking garage with lots of vertical concrete.

After much finagling and swearing, we managed to get the truck jumped. Finally, I got home with my daughter and started to tend to my mounds of laundry. Then the phone rang.

He was stuck at the grocery store and wanted me to follow him to the mechanic. Once again, I agreed. We made the trek to the mechanic and I dropped him off at his apartment. At this point, I figured my obligation was done. Wrong.

Two days later, he asked if I could take him to the mechanic's shop to pick up his truck. This is Minnesota and it was mid-April, so of course we were getting a wet, messy snowfall.... during rush hour! Ugh!

Once again, I dropped him off at the mechanic and said, "You're welcome." Guess what? He called again and said the truck was still not working and asked if I could bring him home. I put my daughter back in the car, and we spent the next two and a half hours in traffic and crappy weather, carting him from the shop to his home.

Of course, I'm happy to take my daughter wherever she needs to go. I am responsible for getting her places and keeping her safe. However, I didn't think when the ink was dry on the divorce papers, that I'd still be obliged to be at his beck and call.

Even though it was a huge pain in the ass, I admit that getting along well means he helps me out sometimes too.

Swipe-a-Date

The concept of swiping for companionship seemed a little odd to me, but I'm an old-fashioned girl when it comes to dating and courtship. A dismissive swipe seemed so rude, but it's anonymous, so I guess that makes it better?

We all know people are meeting prospective dates/partners via online dating websites. I am not immune to this phenomenon, since this is how I met my boyfriend. With our crazy lives and love of technology, it makes sense to merge the two.

However, I've learned of a new phone app for dating that takes impersonal and shallow to a whole new level. It's called Tinder and it's interesting and disturbing all at the same time.

With this app, you peruse the men or women at your leisure (and pleasure). If you are interested, you swipe one way and if you're not, you swipe the other way. It's kind of like shopping for shoes or purses online, except these are humans.

I guess if I was in my twenties, it would be fun to swipe away, knowing this is not a serious form of meeting someone...or is it? Who knows. All I know is it's taken the idea of courtship and flushed it down the toilet.

I'm hoping the next phone app will allow you to select the guy, customize the first date, and have him delivered to your door. Could you imagine if the date didn't meet your standards, you could return him and have a new one delivered in his place? Now, that's my kind of dating service.

Spin for a Mate

This topic is something I am very passionate about. After growing up and witnessing many miserable marriages, I have vowed never to be in that situation myself. That partly explains why I am twice divorced. Neither marriage was good or happy. Life is a gift and too short, so to stay with someone "because you're supposed to" is ludicrous. I've told many friends to get out of bad relationships/marriages, but they rarely listen.

So there I was, eating my leftovers, across from two people who couldn't be in more different situations.

started thinking about this concept again after having lunch one day with two of my co-workers. The one co-worker (a guy) had been with his wife nineteen years and appeared to be happily married. The other co-worker (a woman), was just dumped by an asshole of a boyfriend.

So there I was, eating my leftovers, across from two people who couldn't be in more different situations. We have the guy who is either truly in love with his wife or miserable but doesn't want to leave and the bitter woman who thinks all men suck because her boyfriend claims he "wasn't ready for a commitment."

As I was listening to her talk about her nasty breakup, my other co-worker was burying his face in his lunch. I came up with a "brilliant" idea. Wouldn't it be great if we could rotate mates like the spinning wheel at the meat raffle? Get sick of this boyfriend/husband, spin the wheel, and get a new one! This is a little tongue in cheek, but wouldn't this be fun?

Now, hold on. I'm not condoning cheating or quitting relationships. I'm just saying it's hard to be in a relationship for eight months, let alone nineteen or fifty years. Are we really meant to be with one person? I love the concept of having one person to be there to love and cherish until you both croak, but is that realistic?

I remember being a kid and watching my grandparents interact. They would seem to be happy, but at the end of the evening, Grandpa would go to the man cave or to his bedroom, while Grandma went to her bedroom.

Back then, people stayed together because of the kids, religious beliefs, economics, social stigma, etc. Nowadays, those things still have some influence, but not enough for most people to keep a miserable marriage intact.

I'm not saying divorce is always the right way to go, but I do feel life is short, and why be with someone who isn't going to make you happy? Are we meant to be with a person for fifty years? Are there several "right" people for us or just one?

I don't know what the right answer is, but if I come up with the butt roast on the meat raffle wheel, I'm going to take a chance and spin again to find the filet mignon.

The Joy of the Holiday Merge

The holidays can be a stressful experience, add exes and kids into the mix and it can be a downright disaster. We were finally at a point to begin spending a holiday or two together, but no, the lovely ex had to ruin it.

t was that time of year...the holidays were fast approaching. Family and friends were gathering to give thanks. New couples were dipping their toes in the water for their first holiday together.

This was my first Thanksgiving with CF and his three kids. My daughter and I were so excited to be spending the day with them! Our relationship had progressed to the point where the kids enjoyed spending time together. We were both happy and relieved that everyone was getting along so well.

Plans were made and menus were thought out. All was good, until the ex-wife and all of her jealous, insecure goodness, interfered. As a result, my daughter and I were uninvited to Thanksgiving, and it hurt.

All of a sudden, things are going "too fast" and the kids might be uncomfortable with my daughter and I being there. How could that be when they enjoyed our company on all of our other visits? I didn't understand how this one particular day could be any different?

Their mom, who didn't want my daughter and I to be around "her" children, said we spent too much time over there. This was totally untrue. The "threatened" parent was trying to manipulate the children and use them as pawns in the battle of her will and her ex-husband's will. It was sad and disgusting. And it was hurtful.

My daughter and I had no plans that Thanksgiving, but we made the most of it. In many ways, I was very sad and angry. On the other hand, it was an opportunity for my daughter and I to have a nice, quiet holiday together.

Plans were made and menus were thought out.

We made our own special turkey dinner, watched our favorite movie, and started decorating for Christmas. Am I disappointed about what happened? Yes. Was I going to let it ruin Thanksgiving for my girl and me? Absolutely not!

My Plans for Your Birthday

I'm very protective and possessive of my birthday. It's the one day of the year that's all about me. Part of me felt badly for bringing it up. On the other hand, honesty is important in a healthy relationship.

Okay, I admit...I kind of invited this to happen, but it still bummed me out. When the Minnesota Twins baseball schedule for the new season came out, CF mentioned he'd like to see them play his favorite team, the St. Louis Cardinals.

Of course, the game fell on my birthday. At the time, I said it was no big deal and it would be fun. Then the text came from CF telling me he ordered the tickets. Whoo! Hoo!

Granted, they were great seats and I love Target Field, but it was *my* birthday. This is the one day I want to do what I want, when I want, and where I want. I'm sure it will be fun and we will go out to dinner beforehand, but it's not what I planned, it's what he chose.

If it would've been his plan to surprise me with this for my birthday or plan something special at the game to acknowledge it, then that would've been fine. However, that was not his intention. There was another game he could have chosen but he didn't. Why? Because he didn't want to take time off from work in order to avoid going out on my special day.

I know he didn't do it on purpose to be mean and disrespectful, but it still kind of felt that way. I was mad at myself for not saying something sooner too. In his defense, he was offering to take me out on another day to do what I wanted to celebrate my birthday. It seems that if there is a day when you can be selfish, it is your birthday.

So maybe I have no right to complain? Was Marge out of line to be mad when Homer bought her a bowling ball for her birthday with *his* name inscribed on it?

Happy
Anniversary

I love anniversaries and birthdays. This anniversary was special because CF and I had our fair share of ups and downs the previous two years. Yet, we were stronger than ever and even more committed to being together.

t was our second dating anniversary. It's crazy how fast the time flew by. It seems like yesterday that I found him on match.com and inquired about his goofy username.

Was it all
good times?
The answer is
obviously No.

The response from CF started the dialogue and led to the first meeting at a local sports bar/restaurant. It was great, having good conversation and laughing a lot, which led to a long teenage-inspired make-out session in the parking lot.

Two years later, we still enjoyed being together. Was it all good times? The answer is obviously No. However, the good times far exceeded the bad times. In honor of that, I'm listing some of the great things CF has done for me since we started dating:

1. Opens the car door for me (and other doors as well)

2. Is generous

3. Has supported me through the gains and losses, both in weight and in life, and hasn't once given me crap about it

4. Keeps the number on my side of the mattress at a ridiculously low setting, even though when I'm gone it's like the Continental Divide next to him

5. Takes me out to dinner versus having me cook, even though I've offered a million times

6. Has always been honest, even when I didn't want to hear the truth

7. Makes me laugh and roll my eyes constantly

8. Plays tennis with me, even though I curse at him worse than a drunken sailor

9. Says he loves me first

10. Is awesome with my daughter

11. Thinks my family is amazing

I feel so fortunate we found each other and look forward to the future. Love you, CF!

Why a Ring?

I have been thinking about this a lot lately. Partly because CF and I just celebrated our two year dating anniversary and partly from the fact my former co-worker and her boyfriend just became engaged after a year and five months of going out.

admit it, I am jealous. Why does she get the ring, and the very minute I make a passing reference to it, CF breaks out in a cold sweat? All I keep thinking is it's not fair she found a man to sweep her off of her feet and I found one who wants to sweep the topic under the rug.

Granted, CF has a good reason to be anti-marriage. He was in a miserable one and the divorce hasn't made the situation much better, except for the fact he doesn't have to live within four walls of the nightmare anymore.

For me, my marriage was not good either, but that hasn't steered me away from the thought of committing to that level again. I feel I've found the right person in CF and I want everyone to know that we are a couple. Marriage also means a level of security that the other person can't just run away at the drop of a hat, because there's a legally binding contract.

Wait a minute....did I really just say those statements? See? That's why women want the ring! We want everyone to know that this man is mine and ladies keep your grubby hands off! The ring also shows that someone wanted you enough to get married. I know it sounds petty and childish, but it's a fact.

There is also truth to having security in a marriage. It's nice to know someone has your back and will be there to catch you when you fall. When you're single, no one is there. Sure, family and friends are around, but not at the same level as a spouse.

I started to actually get resentful and mad at CF because he wasn't willing to make that commitment with me. When it started to affect our relationship, I had to take a good look at myself and get down to why I specifically wanted the ring. Was it because I truly love CF, or did I just want the security and the physical piece of commitment?

I realized I really do love CF (I couldn't say that about my ex-husbands) and someday I do want to get married, but now is not the right time. It's more difficult when you have children and exes involved, especially one who does not want me and my daughter around her children. She also makes the kids feel guilty about them wanting to spend time with us, so that makes the situation even more challenging.

I've also looked around at friends and family who have the ring and the marriage, but are still miserable. From the outside, they look like they have it all, but they are dying on the inside. When I see their circumstances, I would much rather be alone.

Then again, I'm not truly alone. I have the love of a great man, and the knowledge that someday he will put a ring on it, just not today or in the near future. That's okay, because I'd rather have him and our relationship the way it is than not have it at all. I'm not settling, for once. I am content and happy.

Dating Tips,

Tricks &

Advice

Confused Woman

You Know He's a Bad Boyfriend if...

1. He is only available to come over between the hours of 6:30 and 8:30pm on Tuesday, Wednesday, and Thursday, which is coincidentally the same time his child has soccer practice.

2. His idea of a dinner date is bringing over Taco Bell for himself and wondering why you're pissed when you have to leave to buy your own meal.

3. Your man's idea of foreplay is thirty seconds of rubbing and kissing followed by, "Are you ready?"

4. His cell phone is always in his pants pocket on vibrate and he's excusing himself to the bathroom every time it goes off, which leads you to believe he's either cheating on you or has "other" issues.

5. You've been hinting for months that you want to do something really special for your birthday. He shows up that night with a pizza/bowling coupon and you're stuck wearing nasty bowling shoes and throwing gutter balls in a dress with his beer-swilling buddies.

6. He says he can handle his liquor, until he's puking out the car window while picking a fight with the Burger King drive-thru employee.

7. You ask for a commitment and he says, "What do you mean? We're committed. I stay over three nights a week and you cook and do my laundry, right?"

8. He meets you and a friend for lunch. After he visits the restroom, he approaches your table with a wet hand to shake your friend's hand with. She's horrified, not knowing if the wetness was water or pee. (true story!)

9. The boyfriend texts and asks where you and your friend are having happy hour. You tell him, and less than five minutes later, he appears. He's either a stalker or a race car driver, considering he lives fifteen minutes away.

10. His main source of income is selling knives on eBay.

How to Avoid
Less-than-Desirable
Guys Online

1. If he has no photo, he's either a cheating spouse, part of a drug cartel, or in the witness protection program.

2. His profile has thirty pictures and ten pages of information about him, but what he's looking for in a partner is blank.

3. He goes on a rant about every woman who's "ever done him wrong," yet says he likes candlelight dinners and cuddling. Um, yeah, right...with a blowtorch and a chokehold?

4. Profiles with pictures of him with his shirt off, with other women, or in a bar drinking. Party boy is not

looking for the wedding march and more than likely, likes the horizontal mambo.

5. If he can't spell worth shit.

6. He responds to your "wink" with, "Hey baby, wanna get laid?"

7. You have "separated" listed as your status on the profile, and he responds with, "Nice, you're not even divorced and you're out here looking around." Like he's the flipping moral compass of society.

8. He responds to your email and goes on and on about a conversation that you and he have never had. You call him out on it and he disappears.

9. In the first phone call you have, all he discusses is his bitter ex-wife and kids and how he's going to be bankrupt for life.

10. He shows up to your first date in a super hero leather jacket and it's clear to you that it's no joke. Would be cute if he was twelve, but he was almost fifty. Yuck!

11. In his profile, he lists his favorite movie as: "Texas Chainsaw Massacre," his favorite food is: anything from a can, and his favorite hobby: watching porn. Run.

How to Find a Good Guy Online

1. Don't go after the first guys that respond like they could be a future husband. The first few I had were complete losers and psychos. BE PICKY!!!!

2. Correspond via the online dating site or e-mail/texts several times before you meet or reveal more personal information. Get to know him first. There's no rush! If he talks about sex within the first few communications, block his ass. He's just looking for a piece.

3. Some women may not agree with me on this point, but I would always rule out men who had pictures of them with their children. First of all, the kids were minors and had no say in whether they wanted to be on the dating site or not. Secondly, I felt like some guys used their kids

as props to show what a "great guy" they were. Really?! Please, keep the kids out of it.

4.   Don't always go for the guy with the hottest pictures. Yes, we are all human. Some of us are divorced and horny. I get that, but I found the good-looking guys were usually narcissistic jerks who would drop you in a hot minute if you were not a supermodel with your thong around your ankles.

5.   If you decide to meet, go during daylight or early evening, and do not let them pick you up at your house. That way, if he's "control freak, crazy boy," he won't be lurking in your bushes long after you cut things off.

6.   Again, some women may not agree with this, but I'm old-fashioned. If he does not pay for the first date, bail. I don't believe chivalry is dead and they should pick up the check unless he's unemployed and you're the CEO of a Fortune 500 company....

7.   It may take a while to find someone decent...BE PATIENT! I went through so many losers before I found CF. I was bored and found him one night while looking through profiles. He had a very interesting username so I had to inquire about it. That's all it took to start the conversation and we've been together ever since.

8. BE ASSERTIVE! Don't wait for men to come to you. This is 2015, not 1954. I believe it is okay to go after what you want. If you think he's cute and interesting, go for it. Now, I wouldn't be a total stalker and hunt him like prey, but a little flirting is great. It lets him know you're interested without being suffocating.

9. Relax! Don't stress about finding Mr. Right, because the more you obsess about it, the less likely you're going to find him. The one night I was bored and didn't care if anyone responded is the night I found my boyfriend.

Confused Woman

What to Do if You're Stuck in a Dating Disaster

1. Have a "wing woman" either inside the restaurant you're meeting your date at or at least a phone call/text away. If the date goes downhill, she can call, letting you know Great Aunt Tootie was poisoned by tainted prune juice and you need to leave immediately.

2. Meet at a place where there's a band or great people-watching. If the date's a drip, you can at least enjoy the scenery or drown out his boring conversation admiring the hot guitarist.

3. A little alcohol is good if you're stuck with Boring Bob, but don't get too wasted. You'll get beer goggles and suddenly Boring Bob will look like an underwear model and the morning-after disgust will not be pretty.

4. If the conversation is at a complete standstill, liven it up with some random questions. It will throw him off his game, and he'll either think you're really clever or clinically insane. For example:

    o   If you were a tree, what kind of tree would you be?

    o   Why is it when I park my new car in the farthest corner of the parking lot, some jerk with a crappy car parks right next to me?

    o   Which came first, the chicken or the egg?

5. The way to get rid of Bad Date Billy is to go on and on about past boyfriends and husbands. Even better, tell him you're desperately seeking out a man to marry and reproduce with before your ovaries shrivel up. Trust me, he'll run away sporting fresh skid marks!

6. If you get any inkling the guy is a loser prior to the date, but you don't want to hurt his feelings, go with this: Show up to the restaurant in the ugliest outfit from the

back of your closet. Don't fix your hair and either have no makeup or cake it on like a Vegas hooker. Have zero manners, belch, and swear. He'll be repulsed, and you can move on to happy hour with your girlfriends.

7. Eat beforehand so if you get to the restaurant and he's Disgusting Dick, you can just have one drink and bail. No sense in suffering through a meal where he discusses his extensive baseball card collection.

8. Meet at a park and go for a walk on the first date. That way, if it doesn't work out, you can say, "Wow! Look at that amazing pine tree!" and run in the other direction.

9. For a real turn off, find out what he hates to do and seek out that activity for the date. It's a bonus if it's something you're great at. Not only will he be mad, but he'll be humiliated because you'll kick his ass in public.

Confused Woman

Where to Meet Guys Other Than Online (Yes, You Can!)

1. Forget about thumping melons in the produce department...that was so 1995. These days, times are tough and bachelors are lazy and don't know how to cook. Visit the packaged and canned dinner aisle. You'll be sure to find at least one bachelor there. How romantic to tell your kids you met while discussing which packaged dinner had the largest list of artificial ingredients?

2. Go anywhere guys hang out to drink and watch sports. If you hate sports, too bad. Buck up and learn to like them, or at least tolerate being around it. If you're like me and grew

up watching sports with your dad, you're golden. Guys will be impressed that you are actually watching the game and maybe know a thing or two about football or baseball. Bonus points if you can name any of the players or know other facts about the teams.

3.   Is there a popular spot to exercise in your city? We have a chain of lakes in Minneapolis that's very popular for running and walking in the warm Minnesota months (yes, we do have months without snow, smart asses). If you have a dog or can borrow one, take the pup with you on your run. The cuter the pooch, the more attention you will get. Whatever you do, DON'T BRING BABIES or KIDS ON THE RUN! They may be your friend's or sister's kids, but the hot runner guy won't know that. He'll just keep running.

How You Know if He's "The One"

1. You can wake up in the morning with your hair standing on end, makeup smeared all over your face, have the breath of a dead squirrel, and he still wants to have sex with you.

2. Your Mom continually calls him your last boyfriend's name and your Dad keeps asking if he wants to go to the gun range for some "target practice," yet he is still willing to meet them.

3. The dinner you worked so hard to prepare is basically burnt garbage, and he still eats it and says thank you.

4. A list of items to pick up at the store can include tampons and hemorrhoid cream and he won't flinch.

5. You can have bodily functions that stink up the bathroom like a sewer, and he won't dump you on the spot (pun intended).

6. The two of you can get into the worst argument ever, yet you don't have to worry about whether he will be there the next day.

7. He doesn't get upset if you want to have a "girl's night out" or spend time alone.

8. You can go out, have your own life. He is not a control freak, wondering where you are and what you're doing at all times.

9. For every ten things he loves about you, there's one thing he can't stand about you, but he's okay with it and willing to accept it. He may even find it charming sometimes.

10. You have the same sense of humor. This is so important, because life will kick you in the ass at times. If you can laugh together, it's a much easier ride.

11. He accepts and loves your kid(s) like they are his own, yet respects that they have a father and doesn't interfere with that relationship.

12. You have moments when you're the biggest bitch, yet he can just roll with it. When I apologize, CF says, "No worries." What a guy.

13. When you've had a night out at the bars and fall asleep sawing logs, he doesn't kick you out of bed. He's sweet enough to go to the other room for some peace and quiet.

14. You have one of those beds that you can adjust the number on each side for a harder or softer mattress. His side is like a cement block, while yours is soft as a cocoon and he doesn't complain.

15. When you attend a gathering where you know no one, and he doesn't ditch you, that's a keeper. He takes the time to introduce you to everyone so you don't feel like an outsider.

16. You can be brutally honest without fear of him dumping you.

17. People can mistake you for his wife or him for your husband and he doesn't freak out.

18. He's there for you when the shit hits the fan...he has your back.

19. You can talk about getting married and having kids and he doesn't sit and shake in the corner like a Chihuahua.

20. He loves you unconditionally. Period.

First Date
Do's and Don'ts

1. Do meet in a public place. You need witnesses in case Mr. Wonderful turns out to be Mr. Psycho with a rap sheet.

2. Don't get plastered. After a couple drinks, all common sense goes out the window. He shows up looking like a troll and two shots later he looks like a Greek Adonis and you end up doing the walk of shame the next morning.

3. Do find a place where you can actually have a conversation. Meeting at a nightclub at 1:00am on a Friday night is probably not the best choice.

4. Don't meet in a group. The last thing you need is friends chiming in or distracting you from really getting to know each other.

5.   Do find an activity you can do together and still have a conversation. Playing mini-golf, pool, or bowling will give you something to do and still be able to talk. The best part is, if the date sucks, you can focus more on the game and reduce the awkward silent moments.

6.   Don't see a movie on a first date. How can you possibly get to know someone when you're staring at a screen and being deafened by the sound system?

7.   Do keep an open mind. Just because you don't want to jump your date the instant he says, "Hi," doesn't mean he's not the right guy for you.

8.   Don't pick a five-star restaurant and then expect him to foot the bill unless you know he has the bank to cover it or it's been discussed already.

9.   Do get to know each other, but don't tell your entire life story before the appetizer arrives. First of all, you'll have nothing to discuss during the main course. Secondly, he'll leave to use the restroom and never return.

10.   Don't talk non-stop about your ex-boyfriend or ex-husband and what an asshole he was. The last thing your date wants to hear is how awful you were treated and that you burned his belongings on the front lawn.

11. Do be yourself. Do not act like something you're not. If the date goes well, there will be a second and perhaps a third meeting. Eventually the truth will come out and then he'll feel like he was duped.

12. DO NOT HAVE SEX ON THE FIRST DATE!!!! I don't care if he's hotter than hell and you're hornier than a high school football cheerleader. Don't do it. You will feel disgusting and ashamed afterwards and worse yet, he won't respect you.

Confused Woman

The Online Dating Virgin at the First Meeting

This is a simulation of a first date between the online dating virgin (Virginia) and the veteran online dater (Dick). They are meeting at a neighborhood pub. Read the conversation below and ask yourself if this is a first date you would like to have:

Virginia: (Arriving at the pub) "Excuse me, are you Dick?"

Random drunk guy at the bar: "I am, and then some baby."

Virginia: (Clearly realizing she has the wrong guy and is repulsed at the same time) "Wow! That was a long subway ride from Jersey. I need to use the restroom."

Random drunk guy at the bar: "Okay, sweet cheeks. Just know I'll be saving a spot for you right next to me."

Virginia: "Great." (Walks away and looks for alternate exits)

Virginia receives a text while in the restroom. It is her date, Dick. He says he will be a little late. *Wonderful, I'm here on time getting harassed by a drunken dude and he's nowhere to be found.*

She returns to the bar but is at the complete opposite end from where the inebriated dude is sitting. Ten minutes later, Dick arrives.

Dick: "Good evening, are you Virginia?"

Virginia: "Yes, I am. Are you Dick?"

Dick: "Yes, and it's a pleasure to finally meet you. I'm so glad the moon and stars aligned tonight so we could be together."

Virginia: "Uh, yeah. It's amazing."

Dick: "We've only just begun...get it? I love the Carpenters. Do you?"

Virginia: "Yeah, sure. They build things…they work hard…"

Dick: "Are you serious? How can you not know the Carpenters? They are classics, like a fine wine, or the Pet Rock."

Virginia: "Wow, look at the time…I really need to get back to my dog."

Dick: "Why? What's wrong with your dog?"

Virginia: "Well, let's just say Sparky has some intestinal issues and I need to get back to him immediately."

Dick: "Gee, that sucks. What happened?"

Virginia: "Last night, Sparky decided that he did not like all the attention I was giving to my pet ferret, Larry. When I went to bed, Sparky went on a mission to destroy Larry."

Dick: "Bummer, so he killed Larry?"

Virginia: "Nope. Sparky tried to take Larry down but in the end, he lost. Larry formed an underground rodent gang and when Sparky attacked, they took him down and forced him to eat a bag of chocolate. It wasn't pretty."

Dick: "I'm so sorry. Will Sparky be okay?"

Virginia: "I don't know...that's why I need to get home. Sparky is my life and I can't lose him to animal vigilante violence."

Dick: "I understand. Can we meet next week?"

Virginia: "I'll have to get back to you. This is a very critical situation. Please pray for Sparky...and Larry....Bye."

Virginia walks briskly out of the pub and is relieved Dick isn't following. She is grateful not only for her creative mind, but that she has a computer back at her apartment so she can surf for another date.

About the Author

Melanie Reitz has been writing her blog, ConfusedWoman.com, since 2012. She has a desk job, but writing, entertaining, and making people laugh are her true passions. When Melanie isn't working or flirting with a guy in the checkout line at the grocery store, she can be found making silly noises and voices to make her daughter laugh hysterically. If you are near a park and hear swearing, it's probably just Melanie missing another fabulous tennis shot and telling CF to go to hell.

Melanie lives with her beautiful daughter in the Twin Cities, which is also home to her hot boyfriend and the Mall of America.